CANDIES,
Beverages and Snacks
Cook Books from Amish Kitchens

Phyllis Pellman Good • Rachel Thomas Pellman

Good 🌳 Books®
Intercourse, PA 17534

CANDIES,
Beverages and Snacks
Cook Books from Amish Kitchens

Hard workers, lunch box carriers, and children who hike a distance to school or the bus stop find snacks (sweet or salty) and

special drinks a happy reward.

Cooks turn out candy, snacks and pleasing beverages to surprise and celebrate.

It's time for a break — or a party!

Cover art and design by Cheryl A. Benner.
Design and art in body by Craig N. Heisey; calligraphy by Gayle Smoker.
This special edition is an adaptation of *Candies, Beverages, and Snacks: From Amish and Mennonite Kitchen*
Pennsylvania Dutch Cookbooks, and from *Cook Books by Good Books.* Copyright © 1982, 1991, 1996 by Good
Books, Intercourse, PA 17534. ISBN: 1-56148-202-1. All rights reserved. Printed in the United States of Ame

Contents

Fudge

4 Tbsp. cocoa (or   Makes about 2 lbs.
    3 squares unsweetened baker's chocolate)
3 cups sugar
1 cup milk or cream
3 Tbsp. corn syrup
pinch of salt
2 Tbsp. butter
2 tsp. vanilla

1. Combine cocoa, sugar, milk, syrup, and salt in heavy saucepan. Cook to soft ball stage (236°).
2. Cool slightly and add butter and vanilla. Immediately pour into buttered pan. Allow to harden.

Uncooked Fudge Candy

1 lb. confectioner's   Makes about 1¾ lbs.
    sugar
1 cup butter, melted
½ cup crunchy peanut butter
½ cup cocoa
1 tsp. vanilla
pinch of salt

4

1. Combine all ingredients. Mix well.
2. Spread into greased pan. Cool. Cut into squares.

Easy Creamy Chocolate Fudge

1 lb. real chocolate   Makes about 2 lbs.
1 can condensed milk
pinch of salt
1 tsp. vanilla
½ – 1 cup nuts

1. Melt chocolate in double boiler. Stir in condensed milk. Add salt, vanilla, and nuts.
2. Pour into greased 9" square pan. Cool and cut into squares.

Rocky Road Fudge

1 lb. broken sweet chocolate
2 blocks bitter baking chocolate
2 cups miniature marshmallows
6 oz. chocolate morsels
1 cup pecans, broken

1. Melt sweet and bitter baking chocolate in a double boiler over hot water. Pour half the chocolate into a 9" square baking pan.
2. Pour marshmallows, chocolate morsels, and nuts over the chocolate in the baking pan.
3. Pour remaining melted chocolate over all. Stir slightly until marshmallows and nuts are coated with chocolate.
4. When mixture begins to set, cut into serving pieces. Then refrigerate. Remove pieces from pan only after the candy is cold and hardened.

Peanut Butter Fudge

4 cups sugar   Makes 1 9"
1 cup milk   square pan
2 Tbsp. butter
1 Tbsp. vinegar
1 lb. smooth peanut butter
2½ Tbsp. marshmallow whip
1 tsp. vanilla

1. Mix together in a saucepan the sugar, milk, butter, and vinegar. Boil slowly to the soft ball stage.
2. Remove from heat and stir in peanut butter, marshmallow whip, and vanilla.
3. When mixture begins to set, cut into serving pieces. Then refrigerate. Remove pieces from pan only after the candy is cold and hardened.

Mints

¼ cup butter, melted
1 lb. 10x sugar
3 Tbsp. hot water
16 drops or ¼ tsp plus 1 drop
    peppermint
food coloring

1. Mix all ingredients together until smooth and creamy.
2. Shape into small balls and flatten with a fork.

Grandma's Molasses Pull Taffy

3 cups sugar
1 cup molasses
½ cup water
1½ Tbsp butter
2 tsp. flavoring of your choice

1. Butter two 9" cake pans well.
2. Cook sugar, molasses, water, and butter together in a heavy saucepan (to

prevent scorching) to 280° on a candy thermometer, stirring often to prevent sticking. Add flavoring.

3. Pour into prepared cake pans and cool slightly, only until it can be handled. Put on rubber gloves to protect one's hands, find a partner, and begin pulling. (Taffy must be pulled with another person as soon as possible because it hardens quickly!)

4. Pull until taffy becomes very light in color, or white, and forms a rope. Then cut with a kitchen shears into ¾ inch pieces and wrap each in waxed paper.

"Two hints— do this on a clear, cold winter night, and store the finished taffy in a good hiding place so it keeps!"

Shellbark Taffy

1½ cups sugar
1 cup water
⅓ cup cider vinegar
3 Tbsp. molasses
½ cup nuts (shellbarks, walnuts, pecans,
or peanuts)

1. Combine sugar, water, vinegar, and molasses. Bring to a boil and boil to a hard-crack stage (taffy turns hard when dropped into cold water).
2. Spread nuts in the bottom of a buttered 9" square pan. Pour taffy over nuts. Cool at room temperature. Before completely cold, mark squares with a knife. When cold, break apart on markings.

Best Ever Caramels

2 cups sugar   Makes about 3½ lbs.
1 cup brown sugar
1 cup light corn syrup
1 cup heavy cream
1 cup milk
1 cup butter
1¼ tsp. vanilla

1. Combine sugars, syrup, cream, milk, and butter. Mix well. Cook slowly, stirring occasionally until mixture reaches firm ball stage (248°). Remove from heat. Add vanilla.
2. Pour into greased 8"x 8"x 2" pan. Cool. When firm, turn onto a board and cut caramels with heavy knife or shears. Wrap each square in waxed paper.

Variations:
1. Substitute 2 cups half and half in place of heavy cream and milk.
2. Coat completed caramels with chocolate.
3. Add ½ cup chopped pecans with vanilla.

Date and Nut Balls

1 cup dates, chopped   Makes 30~40 balls
½ cup butter or margarine
2 eggs
1 cup sugar
2 cups rice krispies cereal
½ cup nuts, chopped
coconut, finely shredded

1. Mix dates, butter, eggs, and sugar together in a saucepan. Cook 10 minutes, stirring constantly.
2. Cool, then add cereal and nuts.
3. Form mixture into balls and roll in coconut.

Honey Milk Balls

1 cup oatmeal   Makes about 2½ dozen
1 cup powdered milk
½ cup honey
½ cup crunchy peanut butter

Combine all ingredients. Mix well. Form 1" balls.

Caramel Popcorn

3¾ quarts popped popcorn
1 cup brown sugar
½ cup margarine
¼ cup light corn syrup
½ tsp. salt
½ tsp. baking soda
½ tsp. vanilla

1. Pour popped popcorn into a large roasting pan.
2. Mix sugar, margarine, corn syrup, and salt in a saucepan and cook gently over medium heat, stirring constantly. When the mixture begins to boil, cook for 5 more minutes.
3. Remove syrup from heat and stir in soda and vanilla until the mixture becomes foamy. Pour syrup over popcorn, stirring to coat.
4. Bake for 1 hour at 200°, stirring every 15 minutes. Then cool and crumble into small pieces.

Peanut Goodies

Graham crackers
½ cup margarine, melted
1 cup brown sugar
chopped peanuts

1. Line a cookie sheet with a single layer of graham crackers.
2. Combine margarine and sugar. Spread over crackers. Sprinkle with peanuts. Bake at 350° for 10 minutes.

Peanut Butter Bon-Bons

2 cups peanut   Makes about 6 dozen
      butter
½ cup butter
1 lb. confectioner's sugar
3 cups Rice Krispies cereal
chocolate for coating

1. Combine all ingredients except the chocolate. Mix well. Roll into 1" balls. Chill.
2. Dip in melted chocolate.

Hello Dollies

¼ cup butter or margarine, melted
Makes 25 squares

1 cup graham cracker crumbs
1 cup coconut, shredded
1 cup chocolate bits
1 cup pecans, chopped
1 can sweetened, condensed milk

1. Spread melted butter on bottom of a 9" square pan.
2. Add a layer of graham cracker crumbs; then a layer of coconut, a layer of chocolate bits, and a layer of pecans. Pour condensed milk over all.
3. Bake at 325° for 30 minutes. Cool and cut into squares.

Sesame Crunch

2 cups sugar   Makes about 2 lbs.
1 cup honey
1 tsp. butter
½ cup water
2½ cups sesame seeds
1 tsp. baking soda
1 tsp. vanilla

1. In heavy saucepan, combine sugar, honey, butter, and water. Cook to 290° being careful not to scorch the mixture.
2. Remove from heat and add remaining ingredients. Pour into a well greased shallow pan (10" x 15" x 1"). When partially cooled mark cutting lines. When cold, crack apart on indentations.

Kisses

3 egg whites   Makes about 5 dozen
2 cups + 1 Tbsp. sugar
2 tsp. vinegar
1 tsp. vanilla
2 cups flaked coconut

1. Beat egg whites till frothy. Gradually add sugar and vinegar. Beat until fluffy (about 10 minutes). Stir in vanilla and coconut.
2. Drop by teaspoons onto cookie sheets. Bake at 250° for 30~45 minutes.

Variation:
Crushed nuts may be substituted for coconut.

Rhubarb Punch

2 lb. tender rhubarb
5 cups water
¼ cup lemon juice
sugar
grapefruit juice
1 qt. ginger-ale

Chop rhubarb. Combine rhubarb with water and cook to a mush. Strain well, reserving only the juice. Add lemon juice. For each cup juice add ⅓ cup sugar and ½ cup grapefruit juice. Chill well. Just before serving, add chilled ginger-ale.

Nutritious Fruit Punch

1 large can   Makes 2 gallons
    pineapple juice
1 12 oz. can frozen orange
    juice concentrate
1 quart peaches
1 banana
3 lemons
1 cup sugar, optional

1. Combine pineapple and orange juices in a large container.
2. Mix peaches and banana in blender and puree. Add to juices.
3. Grate rind of 1 lemon. Then juice all 3 lemons. Stir rind and lemon juice into juice mixture.
4. Add sugar, if desired. Add enough water to make 2 gallons. Chill and serve.

Cranberry Punch

1 lb. cranberries   Makes about 1½ gals
7 cups water
2½ cups sugar

2 bottles ginger-ale
2 cups frozen orange juice concentrate
juice of one lemon
2 qts. water

Boil cranberries in 4 cups of water.
Drain juice. Combine sugar with remaining
water and boil 5 minutes. Combine with
cranberry juice. Add all other ingredients.
Serve well chilled.

Sparkling Punch

1 6 oz. can frozen   Makes about 5 qts.
   lemonade
1 6 oz. can frozen Hawaiian Punch
2 6 oz. cans frozen orange juice
2 qts. water
2 qts. ginger-ale or 7-up

Combine all ingredients and mix well.
Serve well chilled.

Banana Crush Punch

4 cups sugar
6 cups water
1 large can pineapple juice
5 bananas, crushed
juice of 5 oranges
juice of 2 lemons
ginger-ale or 7-up

1. Combine sugar and water. Boil for 1 minute. Cool.
2. Mix juices and bananas. Add syrup and mix well. Freeze in ice cube trays or pint containers. When ready to serve, place ice cubes in glass and fill with ginger-ale or place 1 pint in a 2 qt. pitcher and fill with ginger-ale. Allow punch concentrate to melt so flavors can blend with ginger-ale before serving.

Orange Julius

1 6 oz. can   Makes about 1 qt.
    frozen orange juice
1 cup milk
1 cup water

¼ cup sugar
2 tsp. vanilla
5-6 ice cubes

Combine all ingredients in blender and mix well.

Lemonade

4 lemons   Makes 1 gallon
3 cups sugar
1 quart hot water
3 quarts cold water

1. Wash and slice lemons. Remove seeds. Stomp lemon slices and sugar together with a potato masher until well mixed.
2. Add hot water to lemon and sugar mixture and stir to dissolve sugar and extract the lemon pulp and juice.
3. Squeeze lemon slices by hand to get balance of juice before disposing of slices. Add cold water to mixture and stir until well blended. Chill and serve.

Grape Juice

10 lbs. grapes
2 cups water
1½ lb. sugar

1. Wash grapes, add water, and cook until soft. Drain through fruit press until juice stops flowing.
2. Add sugar and stir until dissolved.
3. Bring juice to a boil, then pour into jars or bottles and seal.
4. To serve, mix grape juice concentrate with an equal amount of water.

Variation:
  Stir in frozen lemonade concentrate to taste just before serving.

Tomato Juice Cocktail

12 quarts tomatoes,   Makes about
    cut in chunks   14 quarts
2 medium green peppers, chopped
2 small celery stalks, chopped fine
1 medium onion, chopped fine
2⅔ cups sugar

¼ cup salt
1 tsp. black pepper

1. Put all raw vegetables together in a large stockpot. Add water to a depth of 1 inch. Cook slowly until tender, then put through food press.
2. Pour pureed mixture back into the stockpot and stir in the seasonings. Bring to a boil.
3. Pour into canning jars and seal.

Hot Punch

2 cups strong   Makes about 1 gal.
   tea (2 cups water to 8 tea bags)
2½ cups sugar
2 qts. water
5 cups orange juice
1 cup lemon juice

Dissolve 1½ cups sugar in tea. Combine remaining sugar and water. Bring to a boil. Add all other ingredients. Serve piping hot.

Mint Meadow Tea

1 cup sugar   Makes ½ gallon
1 pint water
1 cup fresh tea leaves, either peppermint
    or spearmint
juice of 1 lemon
water

1. Stir sugar and pint of water together
in a saucepan and bring to a boil.
2. Pour boiling syrup over tea leaves and
let steep for 20 minutes. Remove the
leaves and let tea cool.
3. Add the lemon juice and enough
water to make ½ gallon of tea.
4. Serve either hot or cold.

24-Hour Root Beer

1 tsp. dry yeast   Makes 1 gallon
1 cup lukewarm water
2 cups sugar
5 tsp. root beer extract
lukewarm water
6-10 dried raisins

1.   Dissolve yeast in 1 cup lukewarm water. Let stand 5 minutes.
2.   Combine sugar and extract. Add yeast mixture to it. Pour into gallon jug, then fill with lukewarm water, stopping 1 inch from the top. Add dried raisins for flavor.
3.   Cover jar and set in the sun for 3 hours. Refrigerate overnight. Drink the next day!

Hot Chocolate

4 rounded tsp.
    cocoa powder
8 tsp. sugar
pinch of salt
¾ cup hot water
3¼ cups milk
1 tsp. vanilla

Makes 1 qt.

1.   Mix cocoa, sugar, salt, and water together in a pan. Bring to a boil, then stir. Repeat two more times, watching carefully that the mixture doesn't scorch.
2.   Add milk and vanilla and heat thoroughly.

Variation:
    Add a dollop of whipped cream or marshmallow on top of each cup before serving.

Peppermint Drink

2 qts. ice water
½ cup sugar
a few drops Essence of Peppermint or
    Peppermint Spirits

Combine all ingredients and mix well.
Serve ice cold.

Pineapple-Pecan Cheese Ball

2 8 oz. packages   Makes 2 balls
     cream cheese
1 18½ oz. can crushed pineapple, drained
2 cups pecans, chopped
¼ cup green pepper, chopped
2 Tbsp. onion, chopped fine
1 Tbsp. salt

1. Allow cream cheese to reach room temperature. Then mix all ingredients thoroughly.
2. Chill until firm, at least 1 hour. Then form into 2 balls, wrapping each in tin foil and refrigerating until ready to serve.

"O-o-o, we like it!"

Easter Cheese

2 qt. milk
4 eggs
2 cups buttermilk or sour milk
1 tsp. salt
½ tsp. sugar

1. Heat sweet milk to boiling point.
2. Beat eggs lightly. Add buttermilk, salt, and sugar. Beat lightly again. Pour slowly into hot milk.
3. Cover milk and allow to stand for several minutes. Stir slowly until mixture separates. Remove cheese from whey with a large slotted spoon or collander. Place cheese in mold and chill until set.

"This is a delicious spread on bread along with honey or molasses!"

Scramble

2 lbs. mixed nuts or peanuts   Makes 8 qts.

1 12 oz. package Wheat Chex
1 10 oz. package Cheerios
1 6½ oz. package Rice Chex
1 6½ oz. package pretzel sticks
1 6½ oz. package pretzel nuggets
2 cups salad oil
2 Tbsp. Worcestershire sauce
1 Tbsp. garlic salt
1 Tbsp. seasoned salt

1. Combine all ingredients in very large roaster. Mix well.
2. Bake at 250° for 2 hours, stirring every 15 minutes. Store in tight container.

"This is a good snack for a big crowd, especially young people!"

Soft Pretzels

2 pkgs. dry yeast   Makes 16 large pretzels

1½ cup warm water

1 tsp. salt

4½ cups flour

Soda Solution

½ cup warm water

2 tsp. soda

salt

1. Dissolve yeast in water. Add salt and flour. Knead until smooth. Cover with a cloth and let rise about 15 minutes.

2. Divide dough into 16 portions. Roll each piece into narrow rolls and shape pretzels. Dip each pretzel in soda solution and sprinkle with salt. Place on greased cookie sheets. Bake at 450° for 15-20 minutes.

Cheese Ball

3 3 oz. packages cream   Makes 1 ball
     cheese, or 1 6 oz. pack and 1 3oz. pack
1 3 oz. package chive cream cheese
¼ lb. blue cheese or Roquefort cheese,
     crumbled
1 small onion, grated
1 Tbsp. horseradish
chopped pecans
parsley flakes

1. Allow cheeses to reach room temperature. Then mix the cheeses, onion, and horseradish until thoroughly combined. Store in the refrigerator until firm, at least 1 hour.
2. Form mixture into a ball. Mix chopped pecans and parsley flakes together. Then roll cheese ball in the nuts and parsley, turning it over and over until fully covered.
3. Wrap in foil and refrigerate until ready to serve.